BRIGHT IDEA BOOKS

IT'S Raining Fish AND OTHER COOL WEATHER FACTS

by Kaitlyn Duling

Content Consultant
Dr. Elinor Martin
Assistant Professor,
School of Meteorology
University of Oklahoma

CAPSTONE PRESS
a capstone imprint

Bright Idea Books are published by Capstone Press
1710 Roe Crest Drive, North Mankato, Minnesota 56003
www.mycapstone.com

Library of Congress Cataloging-in-Publication Data
Names: Duling, Kaitlyn, author.
Title: It's raining fish and other cool weather facts / by Kaitlyn Duling.
Other titles: It is raining fish and other cool weather facts
Description: North Mankato, Minnesota : Capstone Press, [2019] | Series:
   Mind-blowing science facts | "Bright Idea Books are published by Capstone
   Press." | Audience: Ages 9-12. | Audience: Grades 4 to 6. | Includes
   bibliographical references and index.
Identifiers: LCCN 2018035978 | ISBN 9781543557701 (hardcover : alk. paper) | ISBN
   9781543558029 (ebook)
Subjects: LCSH: Meteorology--Miscellanea--Juvenile literature. |
   Weather--Miscellanea--Juvenile literature.
Classification: LCC QC981.3 .D85 2019 | DDC 551.5--dc23
LC record available at https://lccn.loc.gov/2018035978

Editorial Credits
Editor: Meg Gaertner
Designer: Becky Daum
Production Specialist: Colleen McLaren

Photo Credits
iStockphoto: diatrezor, 22–23, hadynyah, 12–13, Ji Feliciano, 7, 28, petesphotography, 26–27, Placebo365, 21, Wavebreakmedia, 30–31; Shutterstock Images: Caleb Holder, 14–15, fibPhoto, 8–9, Jeff Gammons StormVisuals, 5, John D. Sirlin, 18–19, MDay Photography, 17, PrabhatK, 25, Romolo Tavani, cover (bottom), Tony Campbell, cover (top), Yurio1978, 11

Printed in the United States of America.
PA48

TABLE OF CONTENTS

WILD Weather

Some storms are made of dust. Lightning burns hotter than the Sun. Clouds can drop frogs along with water. **Weather** is always changing. It is powerful. It is wild. Extreme weather can be amazing!

One hundred lightning bolts
hit Earth every second.

BURNING UP AND
Cooling Off

Earth's hottest day happened in California. It was July 10, 1913. The place was **Furnace** Creek. The temperature reached 134 degrees Fahrenheit (56.7 degrees Celsius)!

DEATH VALLEY

Furnace Creek is in Death Valley. This is in the Mojave Desert. Death Valley is one of Earth's hottest places.

Despite its heat, Death Valley is a national park and receives visitors.

The city of Verkhoyansk, Siberia, experiences the greatest temperature range in the world.

ICY DESERT

Antarctica may be cold. But it is still a desert. It does not get much rain or snow.

BRRRR

Earth's coldest place is in Antarctica. Record lows happen in a mountain range there. The lowest temperature was taken by **satellite**. It was -136 degrees Fahrenheit (-93.2 degrees C). People do not live there. But people do live in very cold places. Towns in Siberia get harsh winters. Temperatures can drop to -90 degrees Fahrenheit (-67.8 degrees C).

CHAPTER 3

CLOUDS
and Wind

Clouds can come in crazy shapes. Some clouds look like layers of disks. They have been used to explain **UFO** sightings. Other clouds look like they were hole-punched. A brief snowstorm affects part of the cloud. It leaves behind a hole in the cloud.

Lenticular clouds
can look like UFOs.

MOUNT EVEREST

Mount Everest is the world's tallest mountain. Jet streams hit its peak. People who climb to the top feel the jet stream.

WIND POWER

The strongest winds happen miles above Earth's surface. **Jet streams** are very fast winds. They can move at 275 miles (440 kilometers) per hour. Pilots try not to fly against these winds. They fly above the jet stream. Or they fly in the same direction as the wind.

Climbers of Mount Everest must face cold winds.

Dust storms occur
mostly in dry areas.

Wind can whip up sand, dirt, or dust. It can turn into a storm. These storms are called "black **blizzards**." They can happen all around the world.

DUST STORMS

Dust storms happen on other planets too. Scientists have seen dust storms on Mars.

CHAPTER 4

STORMS on the Horizon

A **hurricane** is a type of **tropical** storm. Its winds can flatten houses. Hurricane Irma struck in 2017. Its winds covered an area larger than England. They moved at 185 miles (298 km) per hour.

Hurricanes can produce **tornadoes**. Hurricane Ivan hit in 2004. It created 127 tornadoes. Tornado outbreaks can be dangerous. One happened in 2011. Over three days, 349 tornadoes struck 21 U.S. states.

Hurricanes can cause massive amounts of flooding.

ZAP!

Lightning bolts strike during storms. They are bright and hot. In fact, they are five times hotter than the Sun! They can reach 50,000 degrees Fahrenheit (27,700 degrees C).

Lightning starts in the clouds. Most of it stays there. But some bolts strike the ground. They zap at 200,000,000 miles (300,000,000 km) per hour!

Thunder is the sound caused by lightning.

CHAPTER 5

FALLING FROM the Sky

Rain and snow often fall from the sky. But strange things have also "rained" down on Earth. They include frogs, fish, snakes, and meat. The cause can be a waterspout. This is similar to a tornado. But it forms over water. It lifts things in its path. Then it drops them like rain elsewhere.

Waterspouts are spinning columns of water. The water does not come from oceans. It comes from the clouds.

Most waterspouts form in the Florida Keys.

Most hail falls as tiny balls of ice.

FALLING ICE

Hail is a ball of ice. Usually it is small. It might look like falling salt. But it can be huge! In 2010 an 8-inch (20-centimeter) piece of hail fell from the South Dakota sky. It weighed almost 2 pounds (1 kilogram).

SNOW MOTION

Some people make snowballs in winter. But some snowballs make themselves. Wind blows across a snowy field. It pushes the snow along a path. The snow balls up and rolls. It leaves a trail behind itself. These giant snowballs are called snow rollers.

Snow rollers are also known as snow donuts.

Snow can roll itself. Fish can fall from the sky. Hurricanes can be larger than countries. Weather is all around us. It can be amazing!

Supercell thunderstorms can bring large hail, strong winds, and tornadoes.

GLOSSARY

blizzard
a harsh snowstorm with strong winds

furnace
a structure used to heat things to high temperatures

hurricane
a large tropical storm that includes circular winds

jet stream
a fast-moving river of air high in the sky

satellite
a man-made object that moves around Earth

tornado
a strong column of wind that spins quickly

tropical
having to do with the tropics, the region of Earth near the equator

weather
conditions that include heat, cold, storms, clouds, pressure, wind, moisture, and more

UFO
an unidentified flying object, sometimes claimed to be an alien spaceship

TRIVIA

1. During hot summers in the northern hemisphere, it might feel like Earth is close to the Sun. But it is the opposite. Earth is closest to the Sun during winter. Earth is farthest from the Sun during summer. The distance to the Sun does not create Earth's seasons. Earth's tilt on its axis does. The tilt affects the angle at which the Sun's light hits Earth.

2. Some thunderstorms actually produce snow instead of rain. This is called "thundersnow."

3. Chinook winds blow east from the Rocky Mountains. They bring warm air during winter months. They are sometimes called "snow eaters." They get rid of snow quickly. They are named for the Chinook Native Americans.

ACTIVITY

WEATHER TRACKER

Scientists study the weather. They take careful notes and measurements. You can study weather too. Choose a city in another country. You can compare the weather at home and in that city.

Study the weather for one week. Pay close attention to the weather in your neighborhood. Take the temperature every morning, at noon, and at night. Write down if it rained or snowed. Were there clouds, or was the sky clear? Look up the pressure and humidity too. Write down your findings in a chart. You can include drawings or photos.

At the same time, study the weather in the other city. Look up the weather information online. Make a chart for that place too. When the week is over, look at your two charts. How was the weather in the two cities the same? How was it different?

FURTHER RESOURCES

Interested in wacky weather? Check out these resources:

Jaycox, Jaclyn. *Totally Amazing Facts About Weather*. Mind Benders. North Mankato, Minn.: Capstone Press, 2018.

Kostigen, Thomas. *Extreme Weather: Surviving Tornadoes, Sandstorms, Hailstorms, Blizzards, Hurricanes, and More!* Washington, D.C.: National Geographic, 2014.

Curious about the science behind weather? Learn more here:

NASA Climate Kids
https://climatekids.nasa.gov

UCAR Center for Science Education: Weather
https://scied.ucar.edu/weather

Weather Wiz Kids
www.weatherwizkids.com

INDEX